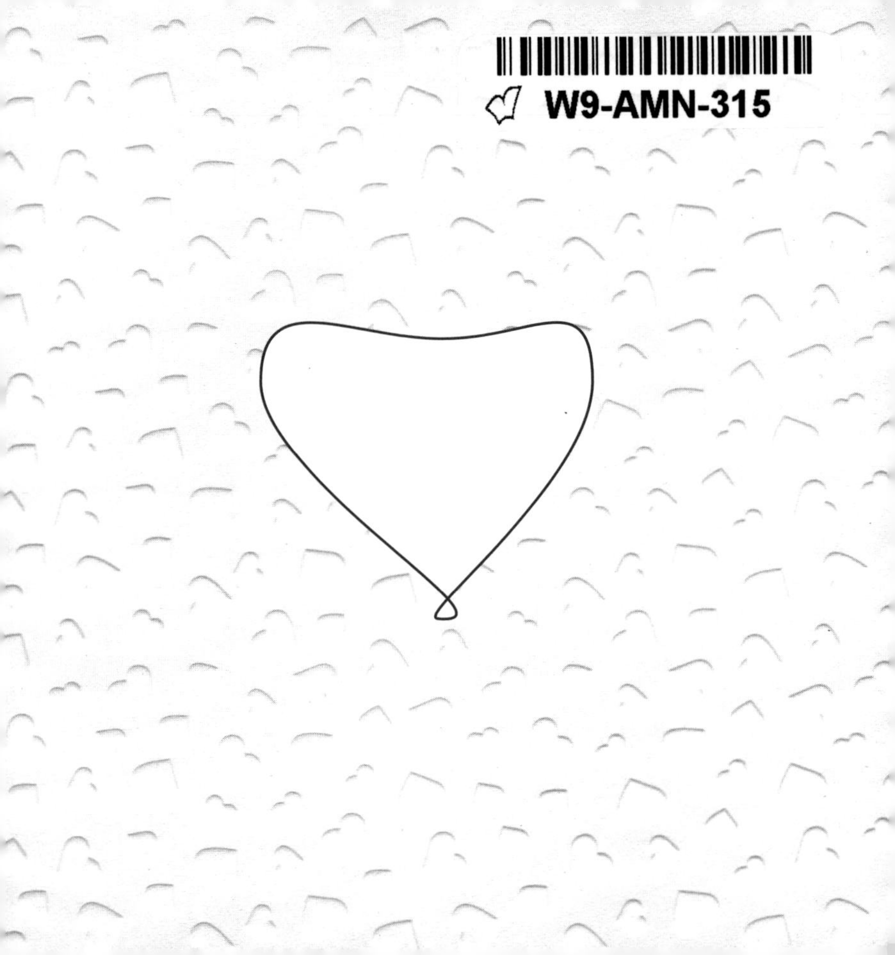

101 Ways to Tell Your Sweetheart *"I Love You"*

Vicki Lansky

BP
BOOK PEDDLERS

Creative through print by Pettit Network, Inc.
Cover design by Travis Fortner

(first published by Fireside/Simon & Schuster 1991)
First edition entitled: 101 Ways to Say "I Love You"

2nd edition

ISBN 13: 978-1931863-50-6

Library of Congress Cataloging in Publication Data
Lansky, Vicki.
101 ways to say "I love you" / Vicki Lansky.
p. cm
1. Love—Miscellanea. I. Title. II Title: One hundred and one ways to say "I love you."
III. Title: One hundred one ways to say "I love you."
HQ801.L295 2009
306.7—dc20 90-26838
CIP

BOOK PEDDLERS • 2828 Hedberg Drive • Minnetonka, MN 55305
952-544-1154 • *www.bookpeddlers.com*

printed in China

09 10 11 12 13 14 15 16 10 9 8 7 6 5 4 3 2 1

Dedicated to the one I love

...

my husband, Stephen Schaefer,
who is very good
at coming up with
wonderful ways to say
'I Love You.'

Love isn't love until you give it away.

Being loved and valued as a person is fundamental to everyone's personal growth and development. It is the basis of our own self-esteem, feeling of self-confidence, and belief in the security our world offers us.

Feeling loved does make a difference.

Some people have been brought up to feel they should hold back on loving words and actions. Others hold back because they've never practiced overt expressions of love, which now makes them feel uncomfortable. Still others hold back out of forgetfulness. We're too busy, too preoccupied or not around at the right time.

We may say "I love you" to the one we love but often, after time, the words become mechanical, as automatically given and received as "please" and "thank you." We may feel we express our love through our caretaking chores, financial support, and companionship. Oh yes, we show it in an occasional surge of spontaneous affection, in shared laughter, in tender moments, in hugs and kisses. But it is the little things we do for each other that show our constant love. The actions. The surprises. Regardless of how we express it, love isn't love until we give it away in real and tangible ways.

Here are 101 ideas to trigger your imagination and inspire you to think of many more wonderful ways to give your love away to the one who matters the most in your life.

Vicki Lansky

Create a crossword puzzle using as clues "insider information" only the two of you know about.

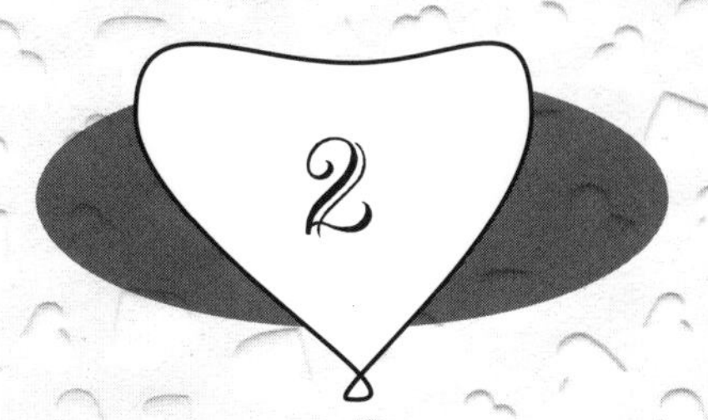

Turning down the bedcovers for your loved one's side of the bed is a warm and thoughtful gesture. An occasional piece of chocolate on the pillow is another sweet idea.

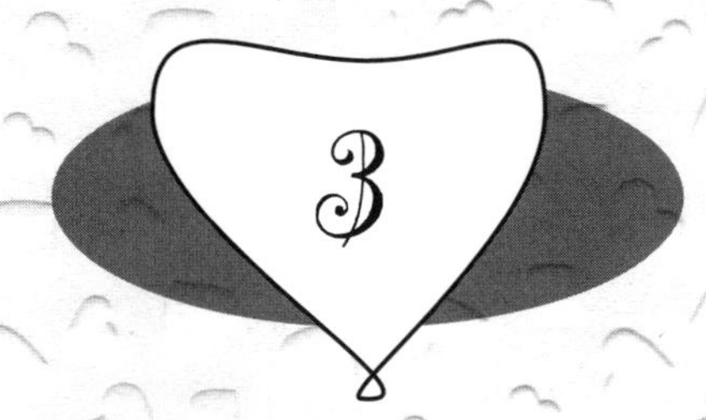

Send free e-mail greeting cards to your sweetheart. Use them for special occasions—or for no occasion at all. (Do a web search for 'free e-cards' to find a site you like.)

Leave a mushy message on a voicemail or answering machine. You may find out that it is listened to over and over again.

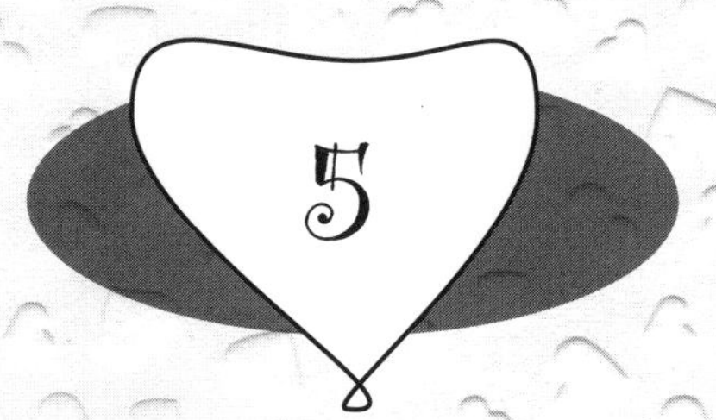

Leave a love note under (or even on) a pillow, in the bathroom, in a sock, on a cereal box or on the steering wheel of the car—anywhere out of the ordinary.

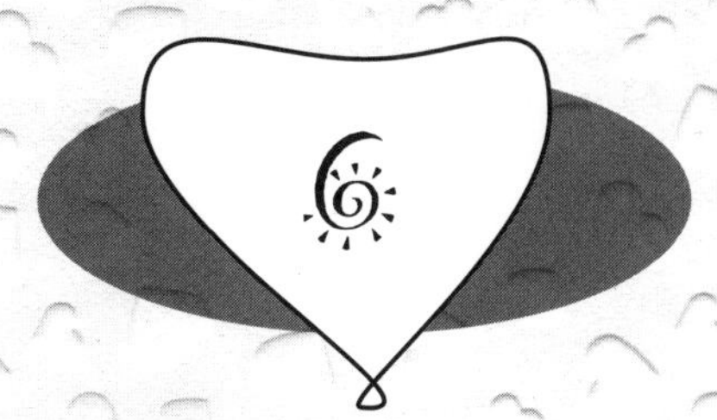

Put yourself into 'listening' mode. Give your love your undivided attention for a specific length of time and don't interrupt or comment. Listen with your eyes as well as your ears. It is a wonderful gift.

Record a loving message and then secretly transfer the audio file on to your sweetheart's MP3 player.

Watch a romantic movie for a 'loverly' evening together. Include a favorite snack such as buttered popcorn or an ice cream treat.

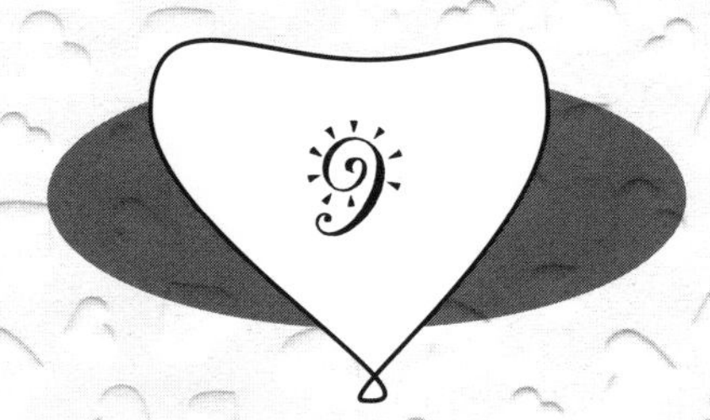

Stand outside of the shower with an open towel as your sweetheart steps out. Wrap and hug! (If you can warm the towel in the dryer first, even better.)

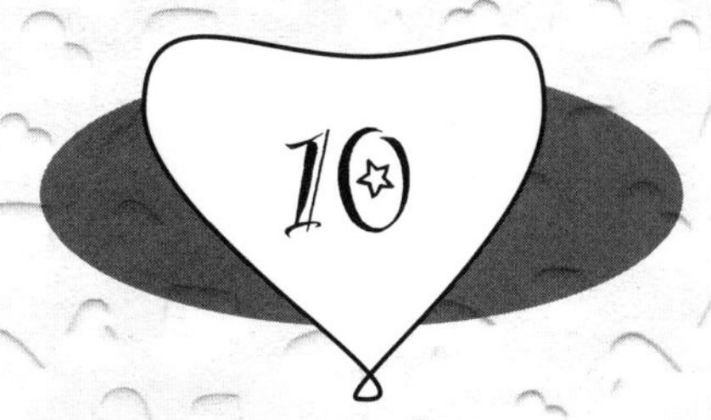

Tell—verbally or on paper—your special person five or six of his or her personal habits and/or character traits you admire the most.

Rent a stretch limousine (when your budget allows) that is stocked with champagne and hors d'oeuvres for a lovely ride, maybe even dinner, when least expected but most needed.

'Send' a postcard while you are both on vacation together (put it on his or her pillow) saying, "Having a wonderful time. Glad you are here!"

Give a 'Love Book' with your special one's name on the cover. A handsome blank book is a good place to start. On the first page write: "I love you because…" Add one idea a page as the days go by and present it as a loving keepsake.

Put together a small photo album or digital clips of your best times together as a memento for the other.

Mistletoe works all year round even if it is only sold in December. Legend says that a couple who kisses underneath mistletoe will have good luck. Hang it over the kitchen sink, from a door frame or carry some in your pocket for use anytime.

Secretly reschedule an appointment so the two of you can have some unexpected time together. Plan something special.

Make up your own personal "I Love You" code that can be used across the room or anywhere: a wink, a pull on the ear, a rub of the shoulder.

Write a loving message on an inflated balloon to be found in an unexpected place—perhaps in the pantry, under the bedcovers, or in a bathrobe.

Lie outside on a blanket together on a fine summer night and watch for shooting stars. Go for a walk in the moonlight, in a new winter snow or a warm summer rain.

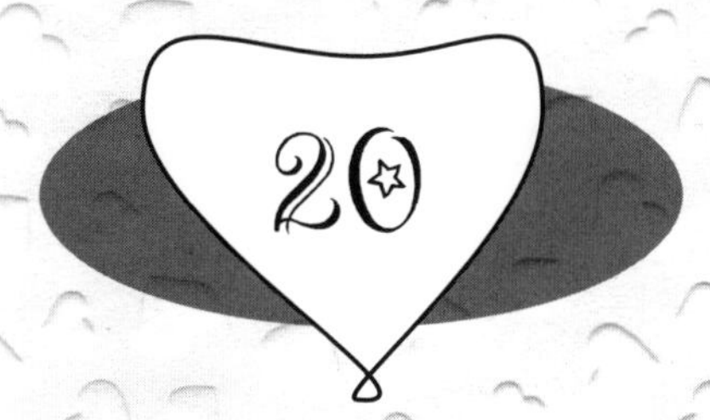

So you hate baseball or the theater. Buy a pair of tickets to your love's favorite event anyway, and escort him or her there.

Write a love poem on your computer and print it out in a script font. Frame it nicely and present it to the one you love—just because...

Make or buy a giant cookie that can be decorated—using a tube of icing—with a message of endearment.

Write "I Love You" lightly with a bar of soap on your sweetheart's car window (on the outside, in reverse writing) as a surprise morning drive-time message. It will come off with a few spritzes of water and the windshield wipers.

Engage in some out-of-character spontaneous play—a snowball fight, a chase around the room or a funny face. Bring out your playful side.

Post a personalized lawn sign declaring your love and affection. You can find one in a party store or make your own.

Take a stroll down memory lane. Talk about or write down and share how you grew to love your sweetheart and what you find lovable about him or her.

Send flowers or a note of affection to your love's mom or dad with thanks for 'creating' such a wonderful person. Your sweetheart will be sure to hear about it.

Deliver something special in a heart-shaped box, be it jelly beans, photos, chocolates or a message. You can find such boxes in craft stores.

Create your own card that says, "What's Love Got to Do with it?" on the outside. Inside write, "EVERYTHING." Close with a loving inscription.

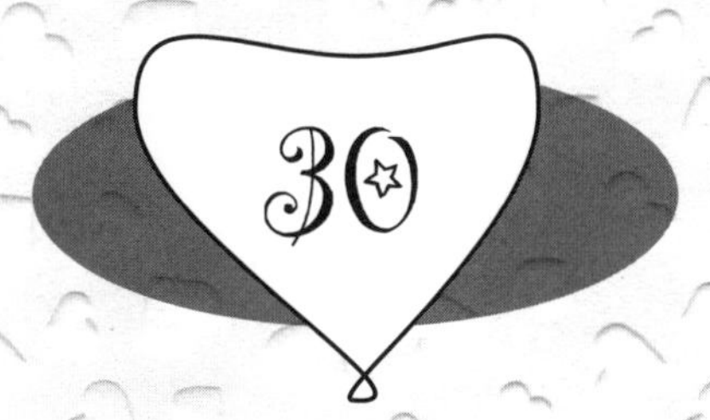

Get a map of your city and put a heart (sticker or your design) over your location with a note reading something like: "Home is where the heart is" or "Love awaits you at 4616 Treelined Lane."

Leave a small bouquet of surprise flowers for your love —in the bathroom, in the refrigerator or even on a workbench in the garage. Or send flowers to his or her school or place of business.

Surprise your honey with a clean car. Do it yourself or use a car wash. Leave a little love note on the dashboard.

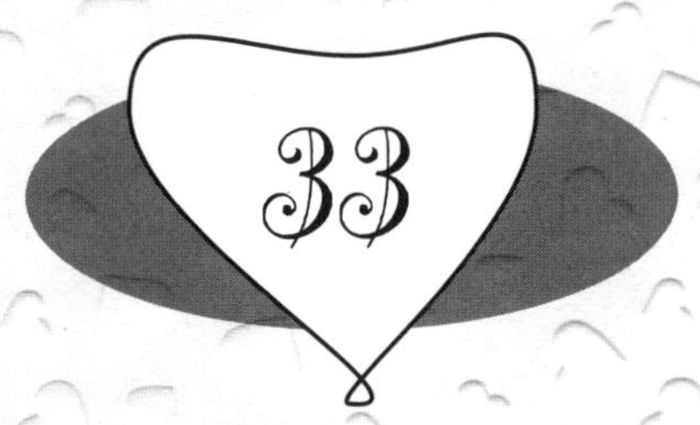

Stumped for an idea or little gift? Look up www.lovingyou.com *for items like glass hearts and carved rose petal soaps.*

Give the gift of a treasury book of love poems with an inscription "To my love..."

Shampoo your loved one's hair. Ummmm. And use a hairbrush to groom long hair.

Sign up for a trial lesson of something new and potentially interesting to both of you—an art class, a cooking class, maybe even a swing dance class.

Take a recent photo of you and your sweetheart and put it into a new, attractive frame for display. Sign and date it.

Send a love song. How? If your computer has RealPlayer *(which is a free download), go to:*

http://minnesota.publicradio.org/projects/ongoing/classical_love_notes/

and you will have many to pick from. Be sure to 'bookmark' the site.

Go for a mystery ride to an unannounced destination. Keep your honey guessing until you arrive at a favorite ice cream parlor, restaurant, scenic overlook or sunset view.

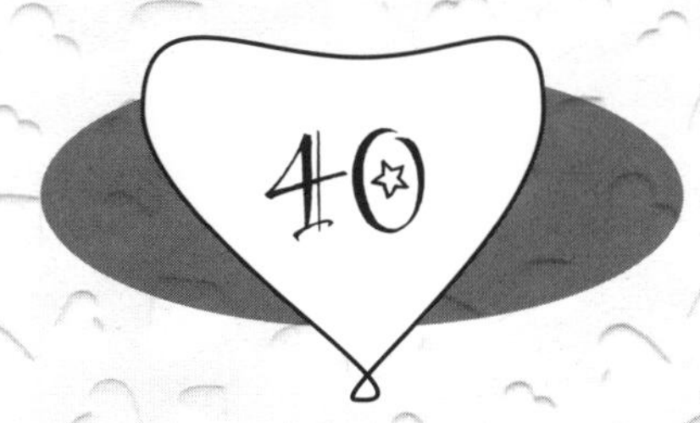

Plant a tree (or shrub if space is limited) in honor of your special relationship. Or give a houseplant with the note, "Our love is sure to grow."

Make a bookmark (with a heart shape at the top or using heart stickers) and write the words, "I Love You" on it. Put it in the book your love is reading.

Cut out a poem, cartoon, or funny saying that expresses your feelings from a magazine or newspaper. Mount it on stiff paper (maybe covering it with a laminate and attaching a magnet to the back) as a symbol of your affection.

Hire a service that will send someone such as a belly dancer or a 'gorilla' to deliver a poem or message to your love's place of business. (No one's been fired for receiving such a gift yet.)

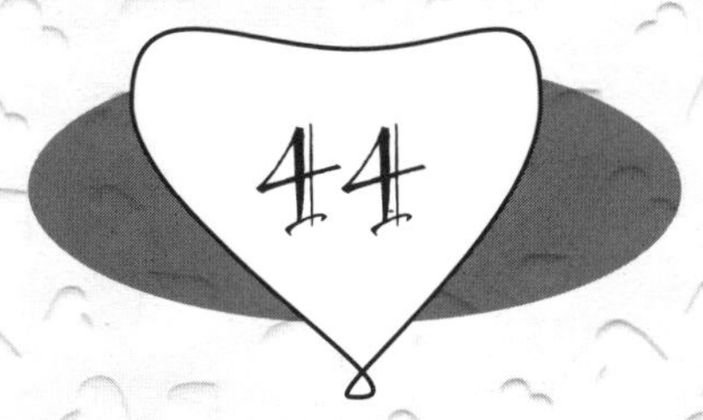

Order personalized M&M candies with messages such as "Hugs & Kisses," "I'm Yours," or "I Love You," from www.mymms.com. *They can even reproduce photos and mix them with messages.*

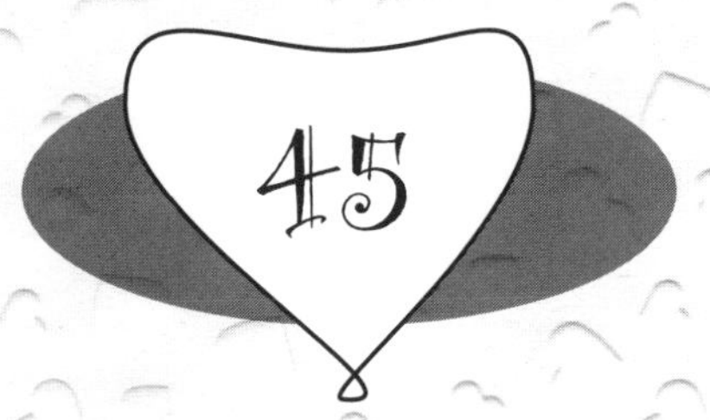

Set the mood by lighting a room with as many small, inexpensive votive candles as you can manage. Or use a bag of 100 tea lights to spell out "I love you" placed on a safe surface or table.

Create your own traditions such as always kissing each other when you find yourselves alone in an empty elevator.

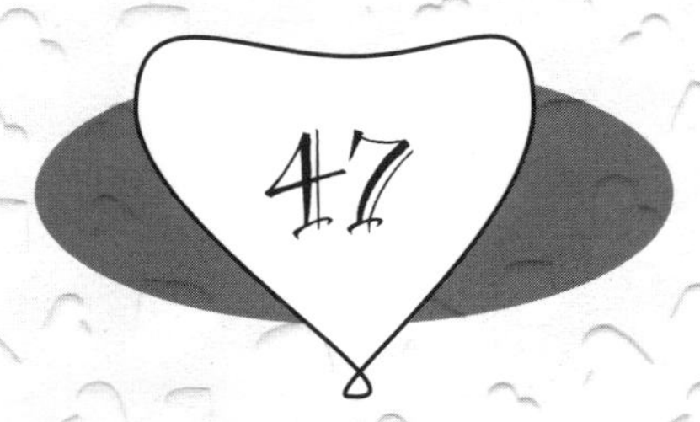

Plan (or spontaneously create) an 'appreciation fest' for your honey. Have friends and family take turns sharing a funny story, anecdote or memory about your sweetheart. Ask that they also write these down. Then tie them together with a red bow.

Send a quote or note "signed" by a famous person such as Barbara Streisand ("Together we make perfect harmony") or Kermit the Frog ("It's so nice sharing my lily pad with you").

Write a check to your love for a million dollars (or some obviously un-cashable amount) as a token of your affection.

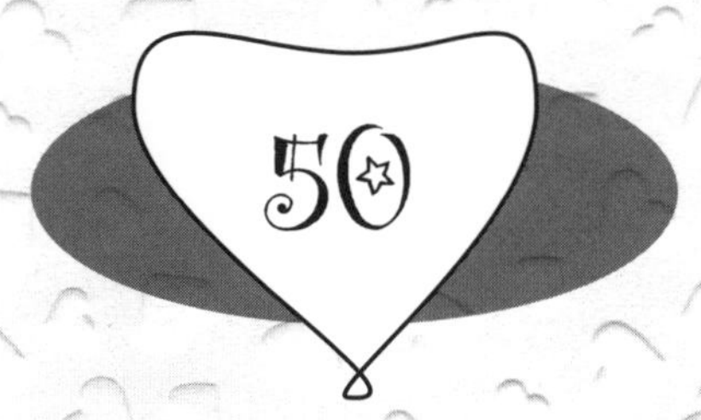

Write the word L ♥ V E using a 'heart' where the letter O goes. You can also dot your 'i's using a 'heart.'

Fill up a heart-shaped box with love slogans. Write 'Rx-Take One as Needed' on the top. Use messages such as: 'Come Live with Me and Be My Love;' 'Love Makes the World Go Round;' 'Love Me Tender;' 'Love is Like a Red Red Rose;' 'Love Conquers All;' 'Love at First Sight,' etc.

Toast each other over breakfast, lunch or dinner to say "I love you" or "To our love" —be it water or wine.

Say "I love you" in another language such as French (je t'aime, pronounced sh'teme). Find ways to say it in dozens of languages from Afrikaans to Zulu at www.LoveIsGreat.com.

Have a meal delivered (homemade or prepared) to your love at dinnertime, or as a lunch surprise at work.

Select the message(s) you like from a package of small candy hearts to place in various spots (and at various times) to serve as your love note.

Call once an hour every hour for one afternoon with one MORE reason you are glad you are together.

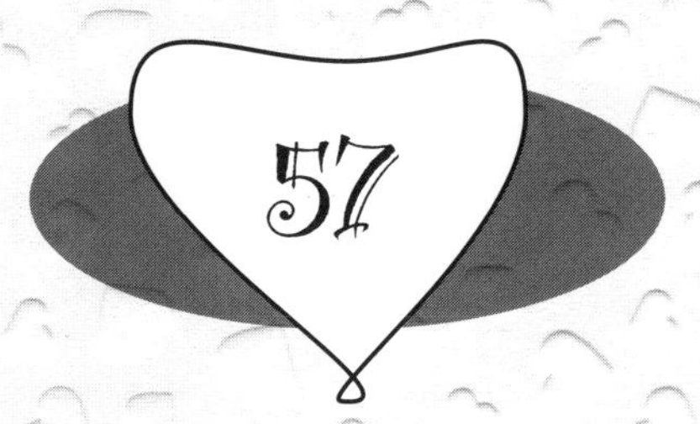

Make a giant 'Hershey Kiss' from a traditional Rice Krispies/mashmallow recipe. Wrap it in aluminum foil and add a paper tag on the top with your special message.

Stomp out or draw a heart in fresh snow where your loved one is sure to see it.

Always say hello and goodbye with a kiss, a hug or some form of touch.

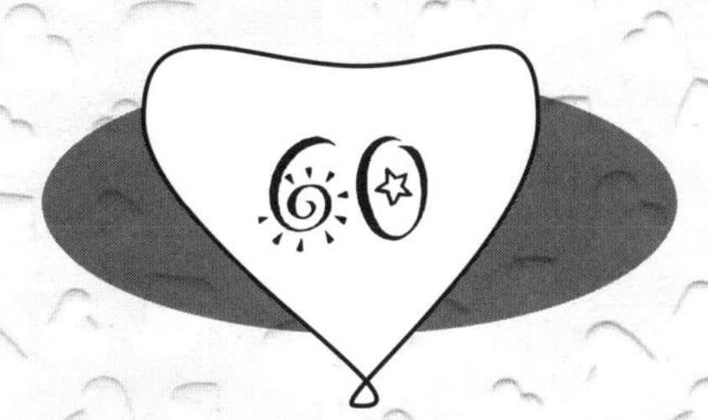

Whisper loving words in your love's ear even if no one is around. It makes for a very intimate moment.

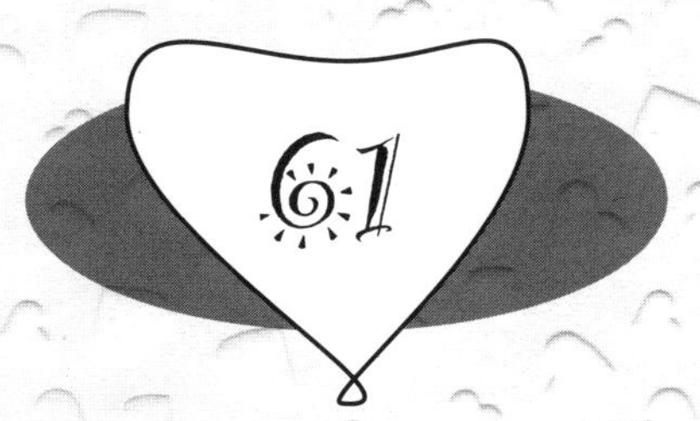

Post a video clip on YouTube.com *or* MyFace.com *telling your sweetheart warm, loving, appreciative thoughts. Then send an e-mail with a link to that page.*

Add a dimmer to your bedroom light switch.

When your heart just swells with warm, loving feelings for your honey, call it what it is—'a love attack.' Then let your sweetheart know about it by phone, e-mail or, better yet, in person.

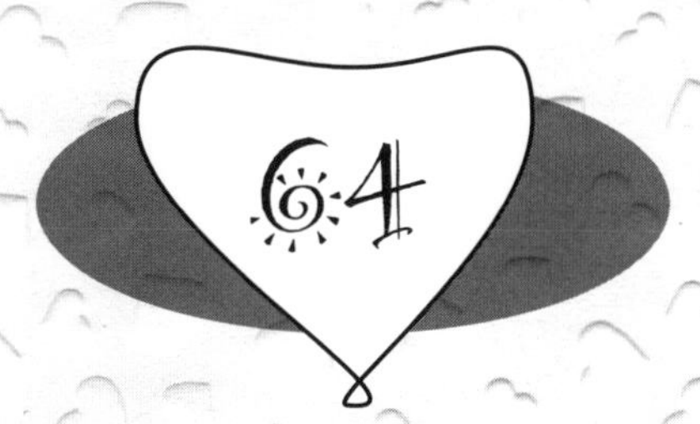

"Warm up" your honey's side of the bed with your body heat while waiting for him or her.

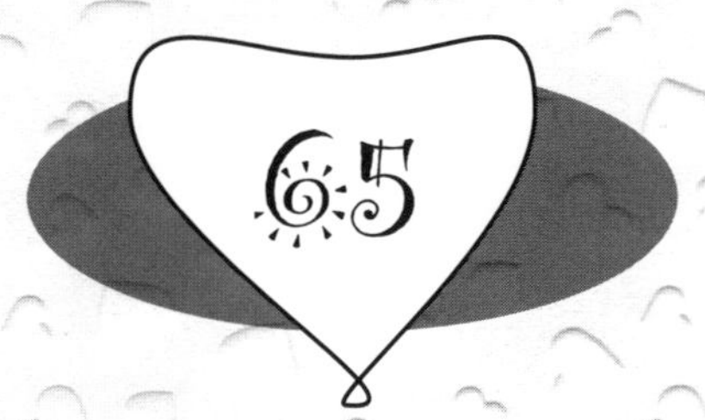

During the next summer rain shower (not an electrical storm, please), dress down and go for a walk together—without an umbrella.

Greet your sweetheart enthusiastically (with a 'ta da!') at the door when he or she arrives home. It's a great greeting, even if you feel a bit silly about it.

Plan a surprise date. Mark a date on his or her office or home calendar that says the time but to check with you.

Create a 'Love Letter' Treasure Hunt. Write more than 5 love letters and hide them in different places. Leave a clue on each one where to look for the next one. The 'Treasure' can be anything from an event to a gift to an idea generated from any of these pages.

Go to a nearby hotel for a night or a weekend and get the best room you can afford. (Places often offer special weekend rates.) Or pick a picturesque bed-and-breakfast inn when going away for a weekend or vacation. They're romantic and personal.

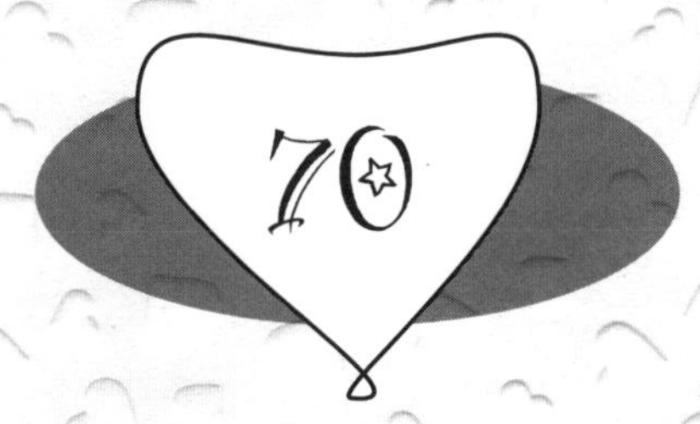

When walking down a hallway or around a corner, pull your honey aside and deliver a spontaneous kiss.

Drop a Hershey Kiss in a jacket pocket or backpack as a loving surprise. (If summer time, pick a candy treat that won't melt.)

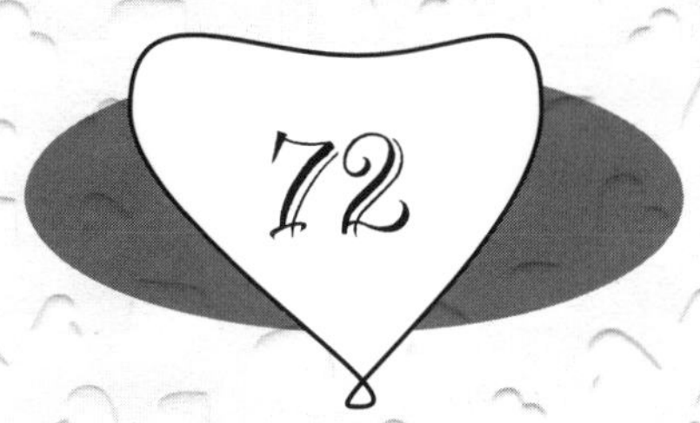

Compliment your love at least once a day about something—anything. Also compliment him or her in front of others when the opportunity arises.

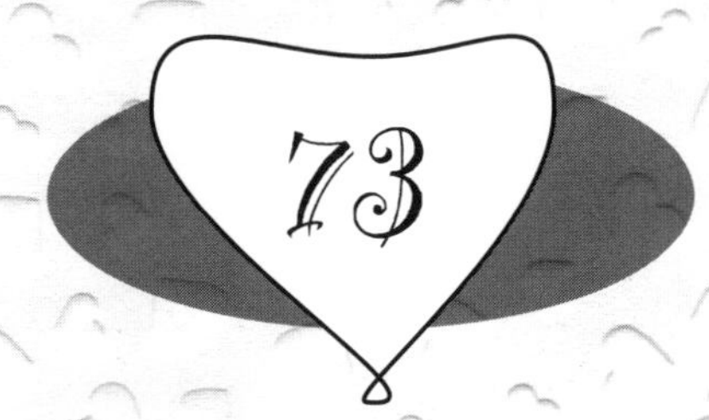

Scent occasional cards or valentines you give or send. Perfume, a man's cologne, even a dot of vanilla from your kitchen shelf will work.

Practice 'competitive niceness.' It's the best way to keep romance and a loving relationship alive. This means doing a loving deed first without waiting for one to come to you.

Spell "I love you" on the other's bare back with your finger. Continue by writing something and then have your sweetheart guess what it is, and vice versa. Good messages are: "I love you," "I want you," "U R the best."

Leave your love a surprise note tucked under the car visor. Or in his or her wallet, maybe even in a shoe!

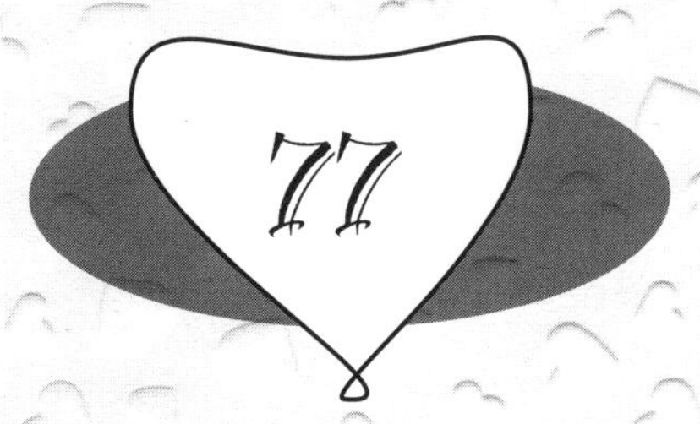

'Write' your love message (or just a heart) with your finger on a fogged up mirror or window in the bathroom or car.

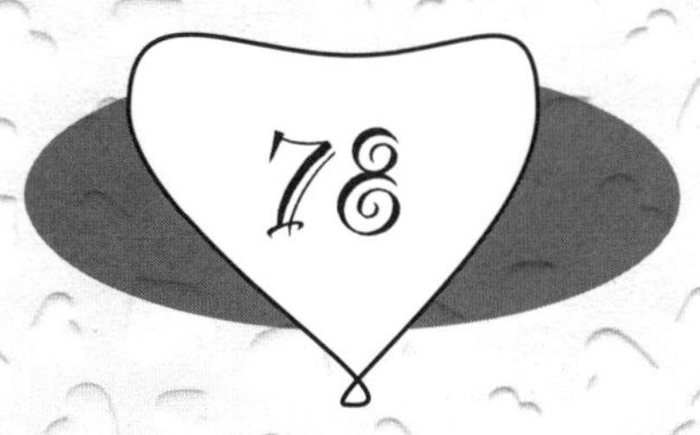

Use sidewalk chalk to write your message publicly on outdoor stairs, a sidewalk or driveway.

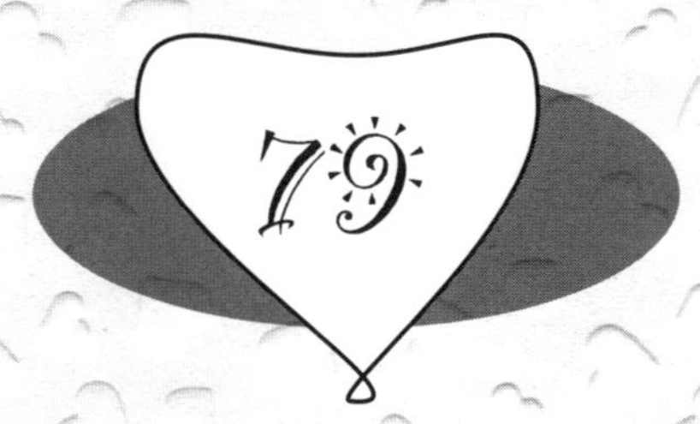

Give a gift certificate for a massage, facial or manicure. (Everyone, regardless of sex or age, loves these!)

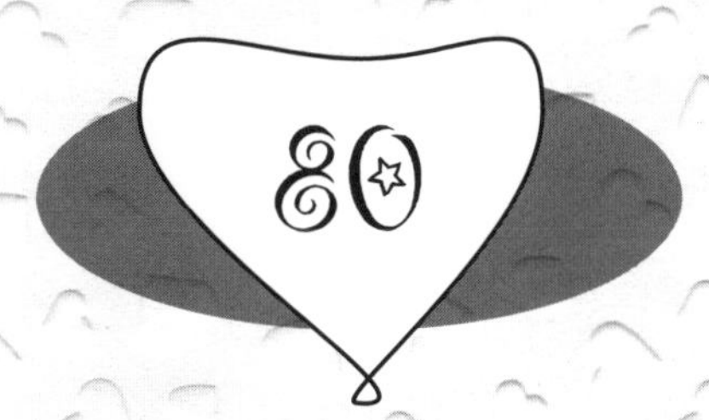

Does your special person bring his or her lunch to work? Slip in a love note. If there is a banana in the bag, write your message on the banana skin with a ball point pen or permanent marker.

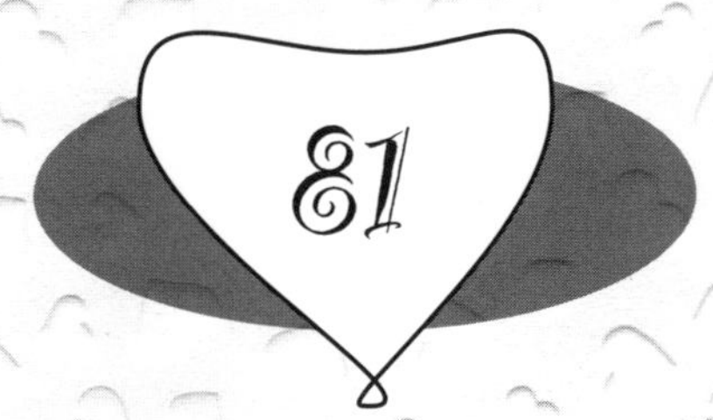

Write your sweetheart a love letter. Talk about your feelings. Mail it (but not to his or her office) marked "personal & confidential."

Give each other "Love Coupons" (you'll find some at the back of this book if you don't wish to design your own)—good for a kiss, a hug, a movie, or anything at all! Use your imagination.

Write a love message on stiff colored paper, then cut it up like a jigsaw puzzle (please, just not too small). Place the pieces in an envelope with a cute message like, "I know you can figure me out," or "My feelings for you are not really puzzling."

A short mobile text message (such as "good morning, love" or "I miss you") when least expected, will put a smile on your loved one's face.

Acknowledge your loved one's feelings, even if you don't agree with him or her. And withhold the temptation to give advice—unless of course, it is asked for.

In cold climates, start your love's car in the morning so it will be toasty warm when he or she gets into it to go to work.

Send your love message in a bottle (any type will do) that could show up in a bathtub, at the beach—even in your backyard.

Hold hands. Hold hands when walking or talking. Over the dinner table or under it. In a movie. Even at a sporting event. Holding hands is good.

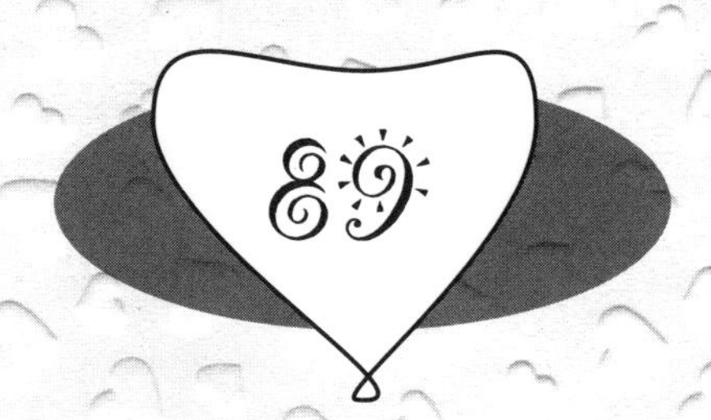

Use a whole pad of sticky notes on which you've written "I love you" and hide them all over the place, or just 'paper' one area. Sometimes overkill is just the ticket.

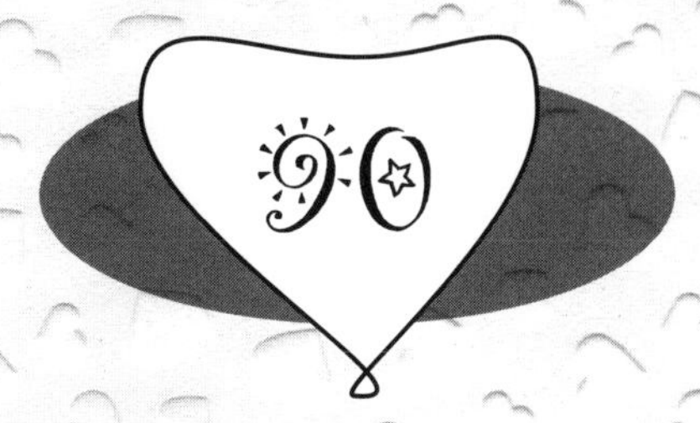

Place an item of affection (such as a glass heart paper weight) in a surprise place ...maybe an underwear drawer...and wait for it to show up in a surprise place for you. Go back and forth with the item but don't let this become a competitive activity.

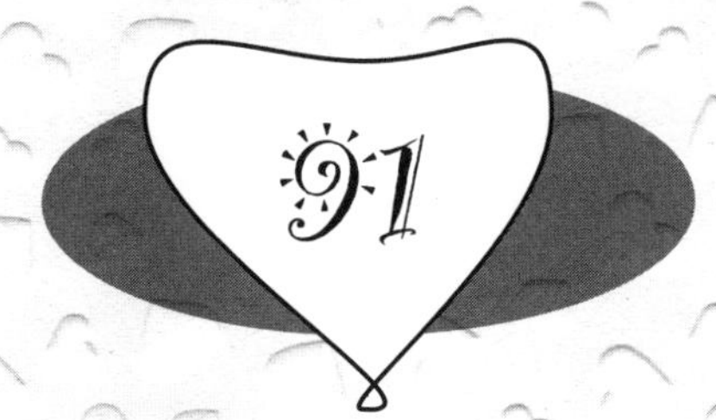

You don't have to actually pay (which you can) to have a star named after your loved one. Check out the sky...settle on a pretty star...proclaiming its new name.

Write your love message on an oversized sheet of paper. Roll it up and secure it with a wide ribbon tied in a handsome bow before presenting it.

Make up a pet name for your love…and use it privately.

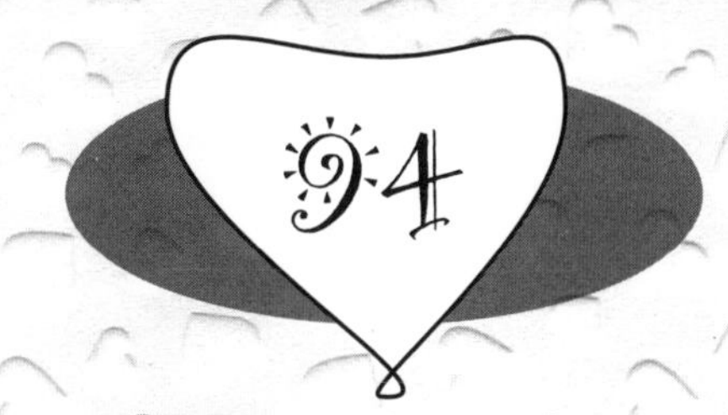

Call your honey at work and say: "Hello good looking! Are you free tonight?" Make some fun plans.

Create a trail to a loving surprise using chocolate Hershey Kisses, or silk rose petals which you will find in a craft store.

Surprise your love with a kiss before he or she can finish a sentence.

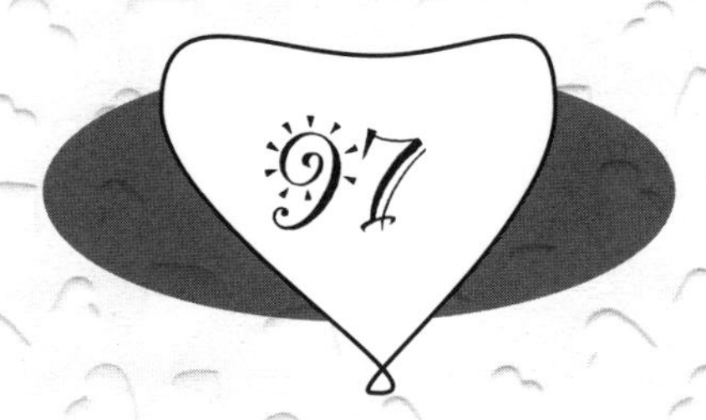

Go for prone. Talking takes on wonderful intimacy when you are horizontal.

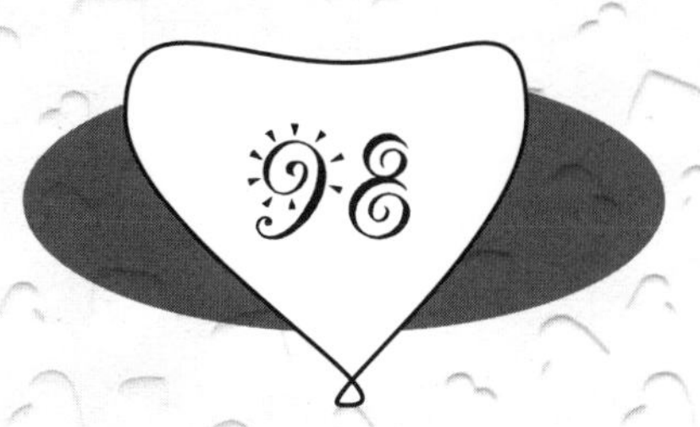

Mail about 5 to 7 days worth of anniversary or birthday cards (paper or electronic) to arrive sequentially during the seven days before the special date. Or have a paper one show up each day in a different place.

If you like to cook or bake, go for a heart shape to convey your message. Make a chocolate mousse in a heart-shaped mold, or shape a meat loaf or bread dough into a heart shape and bake. Even heart-shaped cookie cutters for toast will get the message across.

Here's a nice way to give a compliment: on a lovely day say something like, "Just gorgeous. . . and the weather is nice too", or when admiring flowers, "Beautiful. . . and the flowers are too."

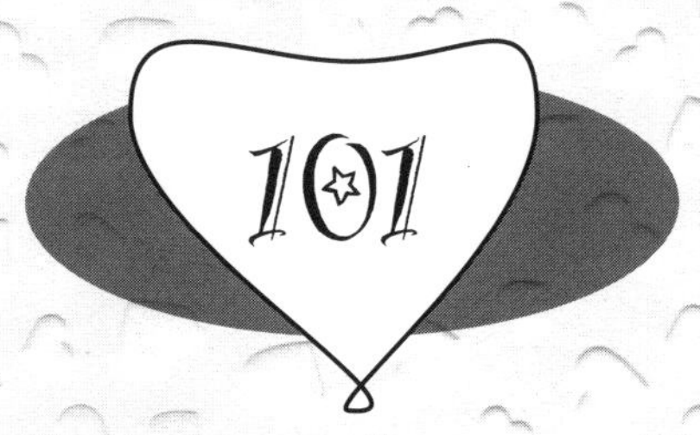

Say "I love you" daily and in different ways. Use enthusiasm. Use passion. Be it be playful, or soulful, try not to let it be just routine.

Here is a collection of words and phrases to add variety to your vocabulary:

I'm thankful for you.
I cherish you.
The thought of you brings a smile to my face.
Lucky me.
You are my sunshine.
I appreciate you.
You R the best.
You fill my heart.
I value you.
You make my world a better place.
I'm blessed to have you in my life.
You stole my heart.

You are my one and only.
I adore you.
You're the best thing that ever happened to me.
You are the light of my life.
You fill my heart.
You mean the world to me.
You're absolutely wonderful.
You're the apple of my eye.
Who knew I'd be the one for you.
Each day I love you more.
Grow old with me...the best is yet to be.
Loving you has opened my heart.
Each day I love you more.
You are the love of my life.
You are my one true love.

Good for:

Redeem Anytime

Good for:

___

Redeem Anytime

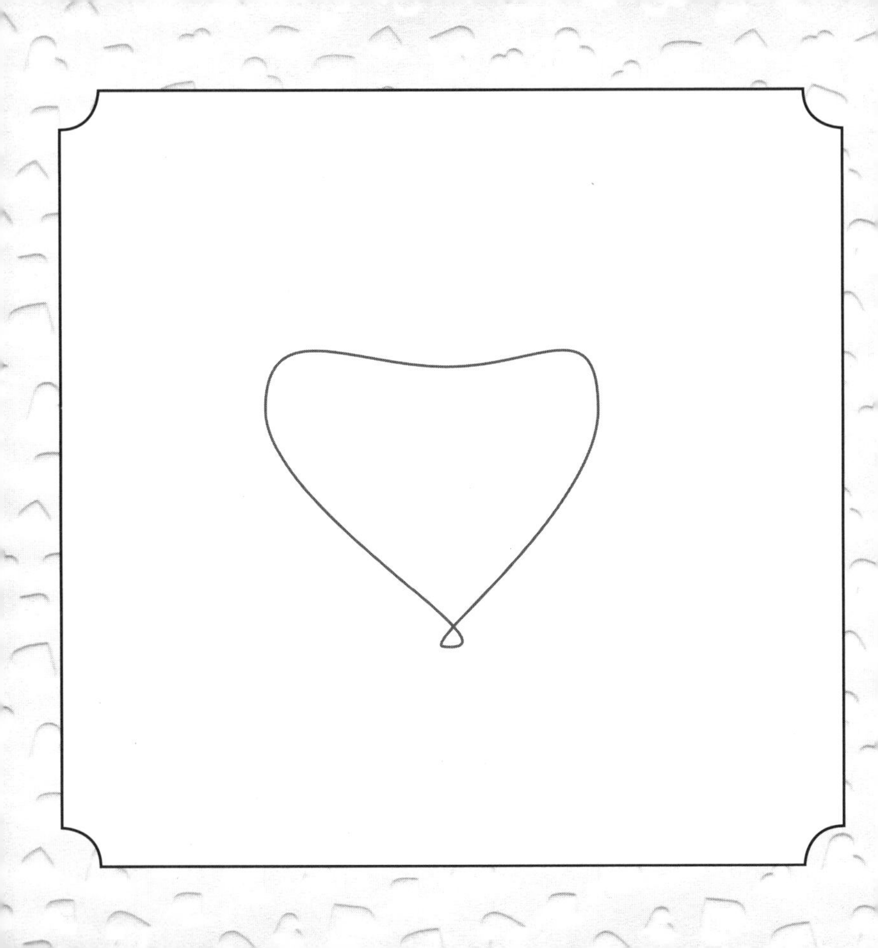

Good for:

Redeem Anytime

Good for:

Redeem Anytime

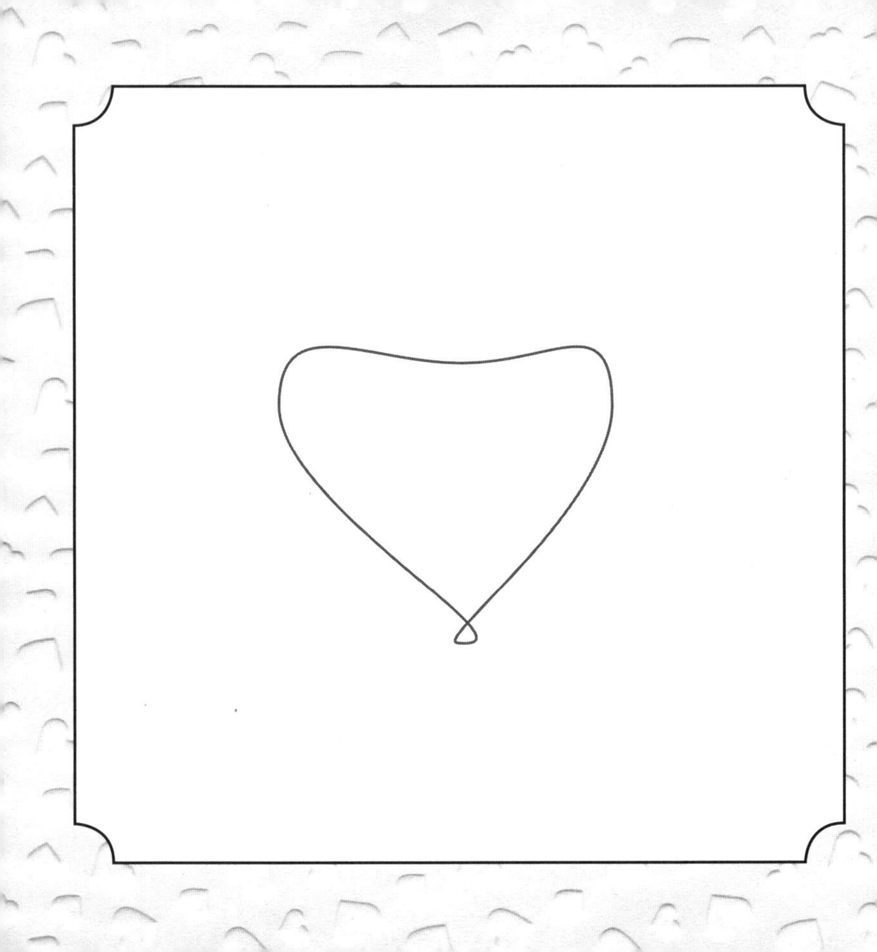

For more information on books by Vicki Lansky, or to order her books, visit her websites: www.practicalparenting.com and www.bookpeddlers.com.

Call 1-952-544-1154 for a free catalog or to place an order.